GET
WELL
SOON

GET WELL SOON

poems

JAMIE SHARPE

With an afterword by
Roote, Norn, and Jasckman

Published by ECW Press
665 Gerrard Street East
Toronto, Ontario, Canada M4M 1Y2
416-694-3348 / info@ecwpress.com

Editor for the Press: Michael Holmes /
a misFit Book
Copyeditor: Jen Albert
Cover design: Caroline Suzuki
Author photo: Deborah Lisoway

LIBRARY AND ARCHIVES CANADA CATALOGUING
IN PUBLICATION

Title: Get well soon : poems / Jamie Sharpe ; with an afterword by Roote, Norn and Jasckman.

Names: Sharpe, Jamie, author.

Identifiers: Canadiana (print) 20230580149 | Canadiana (ebook) 20230580165

ISBN 978-1-77041-770-0 (softcover)
ISBN 978-1-77852-297-0 (ePub)
ISBN 978-1-77852-298-7 (PDF)

Subjects: LCGFT: Poetry.

Classification: LCC PS8637.H3775 G48 2024 | DDC C811/.6—dc23

This book is funded in part by the Government of Canada. *Ce livre est financé en partie par le gouvernement du Canada.* We acknowledge the support of the Canada Council for the Arts. *Nous remercions le Conseil des arts du Canada de son soutien.* We acknowledge the funding support of the Ontario Arts Council (OAC), an agency of the Government of Ontario. We also acknowledge the support of the Government of Ontario through the Ontario Book Publishing Tax Credit, and through Ontario Creates.

PRINTED AND BOUND IN CANADA   PRINTING: COACH HOUSE   5   4   3   2   1

For C. P. Boyko

Contents

I

POEMS OF CAUNTPAUX

I

Every cloud's an animal

Hate the natural

Want puffs of white Gitanes
Then absinthe showers

People in parks
Run by their hounds

We should float away

The factory's smoking

This bench filthy
When I sit on it

II

Death's a can of beans. My death a can of beans. I knew I know what it means. Hosanna. Factories laid it there: starch, pork, and workers' hair. Soupy joy for those with means. Hosanna.

I'm not well today. Mother's on my nerves. She hogs the lavatory.

III

Certain this pine box's
a coincidence

swollen with someone else,

I swung from trees,
swam in seas. Strangled

my member to rid myself

of what I knew. As far
as I know I came

at nightfall.

IV

Gather sticks
into great faggots.

Collect children
to throw stones at sticks.

They do it wrong:
can't win.

In this way it's taught
it's just as just to lose.

(Except Victor in his sea
of black eyes, bloodied noses.)

V

Some beauty got through

Vulnerable to the world

Until the next slight hardens

A plump peach

Tears for trees of peaches

Immobile in the orchard

My teeth pierce the skin

So beauty gets through

VI

Open bakery doors
for grannies.

Knead wives.
Pound children.

Dentures
absolve.

       Doors close.
       Old,

       beat, sold.
       Right's

       flashing
       what's left.

VII

Everything I write's
a love letter
ending,

Hope you die.
Hope I die
in the most

romantic way:
eating cupcakes,*

holding the door
for Ms. Saint-Loup.

---

*   In the original, kouign-amann: a yeasty, buttery cake dusted with sugar.

VIII

Your late grandmother
Visits me

With photos
Of your childhood

I'm in love
Again

Telling you
Is too terrible

IX

For a spell, I
was the world: eyeing,
murmuring, sharing

spirits. Asked for sleep,
but shook scenes from life.
Recalled latkes met

days before and sank
or was thrown. Stuck to home.
To escape I stayed,

swayed, swallowing,
purging, threatening
the air about me.

X

Inability to experience joy
from a meritus eulogy,
praise whispers

as I limp along.
No one screams
anymore.

A hearse, stationary,
spinning its wheels,

pushing more and more
of the world towards us.

XI

Don't invite me
In summer

Late September
Early October

Ten degrees
Light breeze

The sun's
Gentle blanket

Keep handsome
Gentlemen away

Beautiful women
In cardigans

Make me forlorn
Serve me

Red wine
In coffee cups

Then I'll grace
Packed houses

Prepared for
These words

II

THE
HALF
MIRROR

Enderton Glass

If the building had windows they'd afforded a view. The stone square block stood on a rise of hills outside town. Some said it was a prison, while others claimed it an old missionary school, with both guesses being right. From Main Street—where Denton waited—the building's dusk shadow extended past the valley towards Enderton. He stared at the building. It didn't stare back.

Denton worked in most of the shops that sat along Enderton's main lane without gainful employment. He: swept hair at the barber's; removed hot cross buns from the bakery's oven (prematurely & burning himself in the process); bussed dirty dishes to the back of the café; reorganized half the canned goods alphabetically in the grocery. Invariably, when the shop's proprietor found Denton putting himself to use, instead of rewarding initiative with praise and a paycheck, Denton was booted to the street with, "Don't let me catch you here again. Create a mess elsewhere."

"What makes owners weary of their workers?" Denton thought. "Do they find work so distasteful they distrust anyone who'd do it for them?" Sitting on a bench next to the ungrateful barber's pole, Denton gazed at the stone building up the hill. "Perhaps they have need of me there? As a caretaker or interior decorator? I have ideas on furniture placement . . . window coverings . . . if only the place had windows."

As the sun sank, with the stone building's shadow resting against the edge of town, evening's chill returned Denton home. The cottage, which seemed so cramped when his mother was alive, now had ample room for his supply of tide charts and maps, newspaper clippings and expired light bulbs, flower-pressings and specimen jars. In the middle of the living room sat his mother's treadle table sewing machine, the cottage's sole piece of furniture aside from a single mattress. Denton stood beside his mother's antique contraption, pumping the pedal board with one foot, listening to the comforting whir of the machine's belt.

"Purpose!" he thought. "To have a simple, singular function, yet infinite expressions thereof. To the sewing machine: pyjamas and an army uniform are equal; a baby blanket and a shroud were one. To sew is to sew. This machine asks only for a foot to pump it and a hand to feed fabric."

Denton watched his boot rhythmically rise on the pedal as the needle fell. "I would like to build a contraption, perhaps harnessing the cold west wind (which otherwise makes life so unbearable this time of year), that could drive the pedal board and fabric both. Then I'd only choose what the machine made. And then I'd make a choosing machine." These thoughts excited Denton. His foot pumped faster. "People on the streets would exclaim, 'What a cold day,' and I'd shiver in anticipation of what my machines created." The needle stopped abruptly. "What then? I'd be in the same predicament. No, it must be me: I have to decide, power and sew. It becomes a question of fabric. Material dictates purpose."

In the kitchen, Denton looked at his small row of alphabetically arranged cans: Corn, Northern White Beans, Spinach. The beans were troublesome. Was *Northern White* essential— key to alphabetizing—or merely tacked-on advertising? Would *Forlorn* beans come before *Northern White*? In the end he followed the cans' lead. Those in charge of such things must know what they're doing.

Cooking the beans on the stove, however, Denton resented the pressure exerted by labels. "Why do I cook these Northern Whites, for fifteen minutes on medium heat, as the can demands, when they would taste as good both salted and cooled? I propose a kitchen appliance making tiny sea waves, bathing beans, instead of red rings to heat them."

After dinner was polluted by the stove, then redeemed by his imagination, Denton craved dessert. A hot cross bun. But the bakery was weary of him and, less significantly, closed. He decided dessert would be a long walk, skirting the edge of town, up to the stone building.

Walking, Denton tallied everything he'd escaped and everything that had escaped him. Bookending this list was his short stint sweeping the hairdresser's and his mother.

The hike to the building took no time at all, the distance less than the length of a single thought. Standing, with his back resting against the stone prison-school, Denton became the building's lone window, separating two worlds with his thin pane of glass.

Doing My Pärt (2016)

Author's Notes:

1) From 2012–2017 I lived in Whitehorse, Canada. There I was introduced to a commune, called Whiskey Flats, a secretive community relocated out of town when their original riverfront squatter shack community was bulldozed in 1963. During one summer, I lived on their land and acted as resident poet and barber. The hair in *Doing My Pärt* (2016) was collected from every Whiskey Flats resident, such that it could be used in my work.

Film Clips (2021)

> *Like Avro/ I entered a decade's silence—/ Which is to say I*
> *spent The Tens/ Watching Netflix—and came/ Out with this:*

2) Now living in Comox, I'm part of an artists' collective that gets together
for a bi-monthly film club. At one screening I surreptitiously snipped
enough of my guests' hair for the piece, *Film Clips* (2021). Speaking of this
piece at the Rijksmuseum, in response to a question about its impetus, I
responded: "Ik handel in overleg met degenen die ik knip. Waar zijn we
van gescheiden? Hier hebben we een momento mori voor het verlies van
ons vermogen om met Penélope Cruz te daten." (I act in concert with
those I cut. What are we severed from? Here, we have a momento mori,
collectively mourning the loss of our ability to date Penélope Cruz.")

The Ship of Theseus

In the aughts my nudes were leaked to the internet. Which is to say I posted them. Often. I was very leaky. I'd comment on various forums, under various aliases (Fernando Pessoa, Purrssoar888, Ricardo Reis) asking about these scandalous pictures.

After the better part of two decades, the smallest spark arose as to who this *unrobed Jamie Sharpe* was. But, by then, he no longer existed.

Special Agro-Cheque

I'd paint this orchid
Or feign happiness

But it's forging

A fifty billion
Zimbabwe note

Useless

And beautiful
As your promise

Never to use *aubade*

In a poem
And mine

Never to cheat

A wake forms
Behind my speedboat

Henrique

Was the more tender
Lover

The Crusaders

After Shklovsky

During their first arena tour, a heavy metal band mistook each city for Calgary. When, upon playing for the city, they found it was not Calgary, they'd destroy it.

Out of disappointment.

Meanwhile, Calgary exists.

Fuchsia: Purple Shame

Sergei Parajanov's 1969 film, *The Color of Pomegranates*, is now on YouTube.

The film "[d]oes not attempt to represent the life story of a poet. Rather, the filmmaker has tried to recreate the poet's inner world through the trepidations of his soul, his passion and torments."

> Some striking visuals in the original, although I prefer Nicolas Cage's 1994 remake; who does the *torments of a poet's soul* better than Nic? (See below for comparisons.)

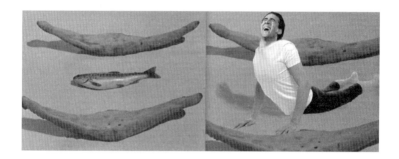

Down a dusty trail on Mount Sinai,
Moses bears God's commandments.

Three millennia later, scholars unearth
evidence of a missing—hidden—tablet.

What almighty words were lost
and why?

Thou Shall Not

A Mark Burnett film.
Summer, 2025.

Half-Life

Pentti Saarikoski,
the great Finnish poet,
never savoured

a Cinnabon;
the confectionary chain
conquered Finland

thirty-two years post
the author's death,
only to disappear

from Scandinavia forever,
like Saarikoski,
a year after.

Invictus

Heaven needs room,
Some space from you,

For you, and for the axolotls.
It's crowded.
We've taken

To wearing masks
To hide frowns

From the landlord.
It's getting expensive.

Now it takes
Everything.

Maybe we should
See other people?

Short Talks on Anne Carson

I've owned my house for five years. We put in new appliances.
I built garden beds out front. Yet the second Anne Carson
languidly taps on the door—thwap, thwap—the house is hers.
It doesn't matter I gave *Red Doc>* a lacklustre review (it doesn't
matter what you think of the moon). I sign over the deed.

There's a rumour I ghost writ *Autobiography of Red*. I'm not
allowed to comment on that.

Sunrise with Sea Monsters

I mourns sweethearts sins.
Begin, without regard
to grammar. End,
hoping never to read
C. P. Cavafy. "Sunrise,
Sunset." Perry Como,
seventh son of the seventh

son, your day dawns on
a vainglorious anagram.
Marry Wikipedia's sloppy
seconds: Brit painters;
Greek poets; Yank singers.
My monster brides, you were,
you people, a kind of solution.

III

POETRY
&
THE
COMMON
LIFE

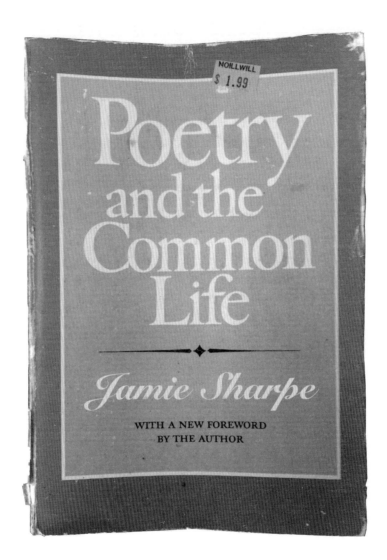

Poetry
and the
Common
Life

◆

Jamie Sharpe

WITH A NEW FOREWORD
BY THE AUTHOR

You got your eulogy,
Lucky corpse.

Checked the veracity of these statements
Against their end rhymes,

Trying to get into space
With my family.

Paperwork errors:

Enjambments, such that

Every time I began anew I'm less
New. Cement, not endlessly handled,
Hardens. See myriad of forms,

But am tired. Don't want to be jostled

Into next perfections—willing to rest
As a thing for next things to walk on.

Writing taught me
To read. I learn nothing

From deer in your backyard
As not to corrupt beauty.

We've ideas about intelligent life.
While we ponder, we're infiltrated

By summer squash on plates
And turn delicious, like

Four line, two stanza
Assessments of Hannah Joan Sharpe
On February 22nd, 2016:

Sleeps
Twelve to fourteen hours a day.

About the size
Of a banana.

Twice now mail addressed to you
Found my home and I peeled it.

Your sonogram's over reliance

On American markets, and dearth
Of Canadian bonds is terrible

Because quantitative easing
Slumbers heavily into 2014

And underperformance of bonds
Last year makes them undervalued now.
Also: patriotism (look it up).

I called your obstetrician.
Hope all's well. PS. Are we
Supposed to be

Checking-in? Shovelling sidewalks?
Wolf-proofing? I foresee

Disaster like Ukrainian
Bread companies shrewdly selling loafs

At 50% off
On April 26th, 1986.
You little turd

In *Ploughshares*. Shit:
Be anal where you dispose of it

As receptacles

Bestow definition.

"Therefore think him as a serpent's egg—
Which, hatched, would as his kind grow
Mischievous—and kill him in the shell."

Considering thinking about
Punching babies in the face, where (heroically!)
I stand against this practice

Unless there's profit in baby punching.
Thumping my wife, the mailman, paternity
Tests confirming

My wife and the mailman.
Suspicion made me

A soothsaying saint.
Things turned out

So I held them upside-down
To confirm I'm up,

As limited gifts believe will
And persistence prevails

Over matters in the aesthetics
Of microwavable potato skins,

Or taters handed to my sister,
The palm reader repulsed

By human contact. She traces lines—
Hearts and lives severed by eczema—

Then cleanses with alcohol. Bills
In her hand touch more than her.

These spuds are: lumpy;
Houses of a million foyers;

Golden Globe Awards for
Best Blurry Product Placement

Going to Ruffles
In *Which Way Is Up?* (1977)

(An image worth a thousand words,
or one sestet.)

Yes, film grows years after words
Wither on the vine, so I drink labels
To understand your wine,

Then invent a not-self to incur
Not right for us at this time.

Better a peripheral pope
To some famous group

Than original
Says the wan poet
Crying on his Fudgee-Os,

Composing
Hooded mergansers
In the Elbow River's shoals,

Waiting to gift
Their terrible tweet:

#BeMyPallbearerTonight

Meaning be deadly professional,
Or an amateur renouncing life.

One's privileged.
One's not.

How to remain
In both camps,

Resting
On a line,

Connecting
You to few.

Tiny Pasolini's
Wisdom grew

Until arthritic
Magpies sang

That corpse
Deaf. We sit, dumb,

Lusting after Cinnabons.

Simple Truth
≥ Bon Mot

Making disproportionate amounts
Of popcorn

While you make all
The money.

Sad

I'm not more
Sad.

Want to change.
Want to chain

You to
Hot air,

Rarely rising
Beyond four blocks
From my home.

Climb to Comox

And we'll go drinking
At the brewpub next to
The seniors' fashion store:

Tipsy on Kölsch,
Trying on shawls,
Replacing burnt

Out porch lights
On burning buildings.

This is a tough neighbourhood
To be tough in.

Scrawling dedications advertising
A forthcoming autobiography:

Honey, Where's the Fabric Softener:
A Life in Poetry.

Or:
Jodi,

You praised me for growing
Evil under your tutelage.

That was youth
Approximating love.

Or:
God,

You've the shiniest showroom
But I want to buy
Anything

And use it
A moment past purchase

Then consider myself
Heaven's great compost bin.
Meaning: I'm alive.

Afterword

Tyran Roote[††], Elizabeth-Murray Norn,[§¶**]
and Yaz Jasckman[††]

The critical response to the poetry of Jamie Sharpe has passed through four distinct phases, coinciding unerringly with the publication of each of Sharpe's previous collections of poems.

The appearance of the first, *Animal Husbandry Today*, provoked what one of Sharpe's biographers[1] has called a "volcanic eruption of plaudits." Indeed, the reaction was instantaneous, global, and exceptionlessly laudatory.[2] Agog reviewers, young and jaded alike, trampled one another—in at least one case, apparently, quite literally[3]—to rush their paeans into print. Any selection of quotations from this unprecedented corpus of acclamation must settle for mere representativeness; to even inkle its diluvian quantity lies beyond the scope of this brief afterword, if not indeed beyond the scope of description.[4] George Melnykovich in the *Latin American Literary Review* declared point-blank that the book "demonstrates that [Sharpe] is one of the world's great poets" (vol. 3, no. 5, p. 160).[5] Maurice Harmon in the *Irish University Review* said that it "comes as a revelation. [. . . T]he poetry is aural and textured with . . . [a] supple control of syntax" (vol. 11, no. 1, p. 112).[6] Richard Teleky in

---

†   Greater Wascana School of Business, Regina, Saskatchewan, Canada.

‡   Center for Research and Teaching in English, Lagos de Moreno, Mexico.

§   Lesser Prospect Hill Institute of Humanities and Health Policy Studies, Cambridge, MA, USA.

¶   Academy of Data, Systems, Society, and Poems, Marshall Square College, Chicago, IL, USA.

** Shanghai Institute of English-Language Literature, Department of English-Language Literature, Shanghai Beiqiao Town University of Science, Shanghai, China.

†† Department of LLLM (Letters, Linguistics, Libraries, and Maps), Honiton Road University, Exeter, UK.

the *Journal of Canadian Poetry* raved, "[I]ts seemingly effortless tone conveys some of [Sharpe's] unsettling vitality" (vol. 11, p. 8).[7] Said Victor Contoski in the *Great Lakes Review*, "One usually concludes reviews of first books with words such as 'developing,' 'promise,' and 'future.' But obviously [Jamie Sharpe] is an excellent poet right now" (vol. 2, no. 2, p. 97).[8] "To acclaim a new poet as remarkable as [Sharpe] is a reviewer's most pleasant function, when it arises," gushed William Meredith in the *Hudson Review*: "This book is a distinguished one in many ways. It is as lucid a collection as has been offered by a serious poet for years. This lucidity, which amounts to a careful and successful attention to the poem's rational exposition, is achieved at no expense to the intellectual or imaginative force. The diction and imagery are strong, oblique and individual, but do not occasion any of the obscurity which we have come to allow as concomitant to those virtues" (vol. 7, no. 4, p. 594).[9] "These are fine-grained, clear-eyed, compassionate poems," wrote Tom Bishop in *Antipodes* (vol. 8, no. 2, p. 164).[10] Karen Leeder in *Austrian Studies* pronounced Sharpe "without doubt one of the most interesting and influential language artists in contemporary [. . .] literature" (vol. 15, p. 206).[11] Jenny Swann in *Critical Survey* said, "If there is a poem in which [Sharpe] sets out to impress, or in which [Sharpe] fluffs a line, I did not find it. Indeed, 'fluff' more generally is not a word that could be associated with [Sharpe]— [who] is about as unfluffy as they come" (vol. 18, no. 2, pp. 100–1).[12] "Across the book's many layers," enthused Andrew Winston in *Chicago Review*, "[Sharpe] takes us [. . .] wandering, pointing out rare and weird trinkets. [Sharpe's] poems are like magic acts, dazzling us with the world's exotica while reminding us that the amazement isn't the point, that while we sat entranced, the real act was going on beneath our awareness" (vol. 40, nos. 2/3, pp. 178–9).[13] Remy de Gourmont in his *Le livre des masques* proclaimed, "[Sharpe] est maître absolu de sa langue; que ses poèmes soient le résultat d'un long ou d'un bref travail, ils ne portent nulle marque d'effort, et ce n'est pas sans étonnement, ni même sans admiration, que l'on suit la noble et droite chevauchée de ces belles strophes, haquenées blanches harnachées d'or qui s'enfoncent dans la gloire des soirs. Riche et subtile, la poésie de [Jamie Sharpe] n'est jamais purement lyrique; il enferme une idée dans le cercle enguirlandé de ses métaphores, et si vague ou si générale que soit cette idée, cela suffit à consolider le collier; les perles sont retenues par un fil, parfois invisible, mais toujours solide" (pp. 44–5).[14] Katharine Tynan in *Studies: An Irish Quarterly* wrote, "[*Animal Husbandry Today*] has every wind of earth and Heaven blowing through it. It strikes you great buffets. It knocks you down only to lift you up again. You come out of it stimulated, delighted, refreshed. [. . .] To the lover of poetry this book will come as a sheer delight. [Jamie Sharpe] can handle the unclean and make it clean reading. It is good poetry right through. [. . . Sharpe] is in the front rank of contemporary poets" (vol. 6, no. 24, pp. 708, 711).[15] Observed Peter Babiak in *subTerrain*, "Poetry, if it's read outside classrooms, isn't something most people like. Reading a poem isn't reading; it's work. And the object of that labour can, to average minds, seem pretentious and self-involved, an unproofed mess of language that pretends to be, through its head-scratching words, [. . .] deep and momentous. [*Animal Husbandry Today*] is one of a handful of poetry books I can think of that are decidedly *not* like that" (vol. 7, no. 67, p. 66).[16] Steve J. Van Der Weele in *Christianity & Literature* wrote, "[These poems] are all rooted in life, in experience, in astute observation and reflection. They shun the tortuous self-scrutiny of so much contemporary poetry. [. . .] Reading these chastely-chiseled compositions provides a pleasure of a high order" (vol. 55, no. 4, p. 624).[17] Sandra Cookson in *World Literature Today* rhapsodized, "[*Animal Husbandry Today*] reveals a poetic language honed to a breathtaking shimmer and precision" (vol. 76, nos. 3/4, p. 78),[18] while Richard Kelly Kemick in *Fiddlehead* revelled in its "snap-crackling verbs, enjambment that zigzags, and metaphors that vault higher than a Russian gymnast" (no. 268, p. 176).[19] Writing in *Room*, Candace Fertile praised "the considerable skill of this poet, a skill matched by a luminous sensibility. [. . . Sharpe has the] gift of making language jump. [. . . Sharpe's] ability to push language to its limits while always maintaining communication is a gift, one that [. . .] readers can open over and over" (vol. 39, no. 3, pp. 106–7).[20] In *Poetry*, David Yezzi, detecting in Sharpe's work a slew of influences, eclectic and eminent, hastened to assure his readers that "The presence of these poets [. . .] in no way detracts from [Sharpe's] achievement. If [Sharpe's] work exists in a fruitful dialogue with such masters, then [Sharpe] very neatly holds [Sharpe's] own, a fact that establishes [Sharpe] as one of the strongest talents to emerge in recent years" (vol. 178, no. 2, p. 110).[21] Gerald Dawe, quoting in *Fortnight* Thomas Kilroy, effervesced, "[Sharpe's poems] enact the difficult in making poetry out of intractable material. The great torque of the style winds-up with shuddering power and then unwinds into relief at the achievements of the poem against such odds. Add to that the sensibility of an artist of exceptional range who has put his own psyche [. . .] to extraordinary test and you have a poetry which [. . .] is epical" (no. 359, p. 34).[22] "For [Sharpe]," wrote Lionel Johnson in *Outlook*, "poetry, the artistic exercise of the imagination, is a safe place of refuge and retirement, a secret citadel wherein the soul may dwell apart for solace and escape from the pressure of the world. 'The consolation of art' is a familiar affectation with many pretenders to poetry; not so with this poet. [Sharpe's] sincerity is evident; it is clear that poetry is to [Sharpe] a serious and real joy, the relief of a quick and sensitive nature, and that the endeavour to write well is both a passion and a comfort. And [Sharpe] does write well, with notable distinction; [Sharpe's] manner, vision, intent, attractions are [Sharpe's] own. Here is not the impeccable dullness of an accomplished imitator, of the soulless craftsman who has caught some master's style; behind or within these poems there is a personality" (vol. 3, p. 587).[23] Fellow poets W. Scott and J. Suckling were moved to rapturously extol the newcomer, contending, respectively, that Sharpe "expresses [Sharpe's] self so well that [Sharpe's] language illustrates and adorns [Sharpe's] thoughts, as light streaming through coloured glass heightens the brilliancy of the objects it falls upon,"[24] and that Sharpe's "verse / [. . .] shall never need a hearse."[25] Summing up for all, Michael S. Ware boldly averred in *College Literature* that this first collection of Sharpe's poetry constituted "a rich mine of resources for future study of a poet of unquestionable importance and value to [. . .] literature" (vol. 33, no. 2, p. 201).[26]

After this copious outpouring of adulation, the publication of Sharpe's second collection, *Cut-up Apologetic*, seemed to catch the literary establishment off guard. As though embarrassed by their earlier unbridled enthusiasm, reviewers now evinced a decided caginess in their approbation—if it was indeed approbation at all.[27] Among the tepid (if admittedly no less profuse) testimonials were Tina Barr's in *Harvard Review*, who said that Sharpe's poems "are sometimes humorous, sometimes satiric, but always written from a perspective which is fully engaged with the world [Sharpe] observes, questioning, inventing, circling [the] subject, expressive of a relentless need to know more, see more, experience more" (no. 1, pp. 203–4);[28] Philip Balla's in *Appalachian Journal*, who committed himself no further than to call the new works "a merry percolation of verbs and verbal forms, turning objects into synapses" (vol. 20, no. 1, p. 84);[29] Donald Hall's in *Harvard Book Review*, who stated that Sharpe "writes lines that look on the page like the poem of our moment . . . But [Sharpe] differs from the others in the care of [Sharpe's] language. [Sharpe] writes with a hard instrument on a hard surface" (nos. 17/18, p. 24);[30] Heather Burns's in *Callaloo*, who cautiously wrote, "These poems are emotional but not sentimental, political without lapsing into scathing commentary" (vol. 16, no. 3, p. 729);[31] Chris Van Rompaey's in *Australasian Journal of American Studies*, who called the poems, "with their thematic diversity and frequent instances of biting social critique ... anything but aridly formal" (vol. 28, no. 1, p. 156);[32] Lee Oser's in *World Literature Today*, who, observing that Sharpe "revels in a world of imaginative memory," and that Sharpe's "range of sympathies is superbly refined and subtly limited," made so bold as to affirm that Sharpe "achieves a very good deal" (vol. 71, no. 3, p. 594);[33] Mary Salmon's in *University Review*, who, circumspectly characterizing the poet, wrote that though Sharpe "is sometimes a calm prophet, more often [Sharpe] is the vociferous chairman of the variety theatre" (vol. 5, no. 2, p. 262);[34] Edward H. Dewey's in the *New England Quarterly*, who asserted, "It is impossible to make prose out of most of these poems" (vol. 1, no. 4, p. 570);[35] Donald Allen Young's in *Canadian Slavonic Papers / Revue canadienne des slavistes*, who, comparatively ebullient, wrote, "Although [Sharpe] no doubt goes too far for many people's taste, [...] the resulting 'exercises' are highly provocative and should be of interest to readers of a variety of theoretical persuasions" (vol. 21, no. 4, p. 559);[36] Kristina Marie Darling's in *Colorado Review*, who, seeming to find greater safety in description than appraisal, said, "Often forging connections between dissimilar ideas through a repetition of words and sounds, the poems in [*Cut-up Apologetic*] retain a stream of consciousness quality, which suits the book's subject perfectly. Throughout the volume, these stylistic decisions mirror the poet's interest in the ways language shapes human thought and how its influence in turn guides one's perception of the world" (vol. 38, no. 1, p. 171);[37] Frank McConnell's in the *Wilson Quarterly*, who claimed to perceive that Sharpe's "attention [is] fixed on [...] the ways in which poetry can make our lives not just tolerable" (vol. 3, no. 1, p. 144);[38] Anne M. Blythe's in the *South Carolina Historical Magazine*, who opined, "[T]here is much autobiography in these poems. [... Sharpe] clearly believe[s] in the universality of [Sharpe's] own joys and sorrows" (vol. 92, no. 4, p. 283);[39] Jerry Harp's in the *Iowa Review*, who noncommittally wrote, "At once skeptical and mystical, as well as both poignant and humorous in the midst of tragedy, [Sharpe's] poems constitute a surrealism that ranges through history and thereby illuminates the struggles and pressures of the present moment" (vol. 34, no. 2, p. 175);[40] James Hoggard's in *Translation Review*, who vouchsafed to allege, "[Sharpe is] a valuable and generous literary presence" (vol. 71, no. 1, p. 64);[41] Virgil Nemoianu's in *Slavic Review*, who called Sharpe's poetry "fortunately rather easy to translate" (vol. 42, no. 4, p. 737);[42] Henry W. Wells's in the *William and Mary Quarterly*, who wrote, "The book is singularly unpretentious. Needless to say, it is not great. But it has substantial, lasting worth and considerable charm" (vol. 3, no. 3, p. 440);[43] Richard Le Gallienne's in the *North American Review*, who declared the collection "surprisingly various": "I have seldom read one book [...] in which so many different things are done" (vol. 183, no. 604, p. 1180);[44] Arthur Terry's in the *Modern Language Review*, who graciously declared that Sharpe's book deserved "every success, not the least because of its very attractive presentation" (vol. 63, no. 1, p. 278);[45] Kay Winters's in the *Reader Teacher*, who elusively said, "This is a somber collection of poignant poems of feeling [...] The language is simple and sparse, brushing feelings, expressions and moods in velvet. The poems are perfect for the days when the sun is too loud and the reader eases into half-tones seeking someone who's been there" (vol. 32, no. 8, p. 978);[46] Peter Stitt's in the *Georgia Review*, who wrote, "[Sharpe's] chief preoccupation as poet is with words rather than with meaning. Given this fact, [...] it would not be amiss to say that [Sharpe] is the equivalent in poetry of the abstract expressionists in painting" (vol. 32, no. 4, p. 941);[47] Carol Moldaw's in the *Antioch Review*, who said that "[Sharpe's] intricate sometimes ornate style, [...] elaborate metaphors and extended sinewy syntax, [and] erudition" all contributed "to a sense of encompassing interconnectedness and inexorability" (vol. 59, no. 3, p. 638);[48] Nita Schecht's in *Bridges*, who professed, "Specificity and contingency—both temporal and geographic—are central to the poetics of this collection" (vol. 12, no. 1, pp. 127–8);[49] Harry Vandervlist's in the *Dictionary of Literary Biography*, who, taking refuge in an overview of other reviewers' opinions, remarked that critical reaction was "divided between admiration for the promise displayed in many of the poems and exasperation at an overexuberant indulgence in word-play and intellectual associations" (vol. 334, p. 277);[50] Emily Bednarz's in *Arc Poetry Magazine*, who said that "Through this collection, one can chart [Sharpe's] de- and re-construction of traditional lyricism" (vol. 82, p. 151);[51] Clyde V. Williams's in the *South Central Bulletin*, who pointedly called the book "the work of a minor, but interesting, poet" (vol. 33, no. 1, p. 32);[52] the anonymous editors' in the *Downside Review*, who announced, "A very dainty little volume of verse has come to us [. . .] It will be read and re-read by those who can appreciate such work, and will, we trust, be followed by much more of its kind. We recommend it as a New Year's gift" (vol. 32, no. 3, p. 356);[53] and finally, but by no means exhaustively, Sesshu Foster's in *Feminist Review*, who likewise deigned, "It could also be recommended to your local bookstore as an item to stock" (no. 24, p. 120).[54]

This "critical circumspection, verging almost on consternation" (as one literary historian has put it),[55] extended even to the poems' substance: reviewers contradicted one another, and frequently enough themselves, in the simplest matters of explication, categorization, and fact. Thus, for example, A. Irwin Shone, in *Hispania*, detected "the dominant note" of Sharpe's poems, "recurring again and again like a refrain," to be "not that of love, not that of pain, but the intense joy of the creative artist which gleams even through sorrow" (vol. 13, no. 6, p. 484),[56] while Anthony J. Klančar, in *Books Abroad*, described a "confess[ion] in pure lyrical verse [of Sharpe's] boundless love of life and nature [. . .] In [Sharpe's] verse we have the tenderest expression of a [human] soul" (vol. 11, no. 4, p. 512).[57] Geoffrey Lindsay, writing in the *Journal of Canadian Poetry*, perceived "a poetry of possibility, in contrast to a poetry of commentary. [Sharpe's] poems are less 'about something,' and more about a state of mind that is the occasion for beholding in unusual ways" (vol. 15, p. 23),[58] while Mary Doyle Curran, in the *Massachusetts Review*, discovered "autobiographical poems that ache with the anguish of a [person] possessed, driven and demented. The past hangs over [Sharpe] with blinding darkness; [Sharpe is] coffined by a self that is haunted by that past" (vol. 6, no. 2, p. 411).[59] Varun Kumar in *Australasian Psychiatry* described the poems as "short, and communicated [in] a stream of consciousness, which means that the author's 'voice' has a clarity and consistency throughout the work. The result is poems which are deceptively simple, but still able to convey profound ideas whilst also being easily understood" (vol. 26, no. 3, p. 323),[60] and, likewise, Ellen Clare Connellee, in *Bios*, called the book's style "simple and refreshing" (vol. 3, no. 2, p. 114);[61] Jack Shreve and Robert Colucci, however, writing in the *Critical Survey of Poetry: Topical Essays*, found in the work "a surface difficulty, a highly condensed but personal symbolism suggesting the need to penetrate appearances in order to apprehend the real. [. . . A]ccess to the real is permitted only by linguistic experimentation, for the language of everyday usage has been enslaved for superficial, purely utilitarian ends [. . .] At its most radical, [*Cut-up Apologetic*] virtually eschews content, suggesting the fragmentation, asymmetry, and nonnaturalism of much modern music" (vol. 1, pp. 409–10).[62] While Regina Grol-Prokopczyk, writing in the *Polish Review*, saw in Sharpe a poet who "contemplates the multiplicity of human motives, shows great sensitivity to problems of aging, marital tensions and, overall, the impact of external determinants on one's life" (vol. 27, nos. 3/4, p. 223),[63] Peter T. Koper, in *Michigan Historical Review*, recognized instead poems that "record the mix of images, associations, rituals, skills, and longings that give fly fishing so much depth of meaning" (vol. 19, no. 1, p. 71).[64] Hermann Binder, in *Literarische Warte: Monatsschrift für Schöne Literatur*, wrote, "Dieser [. . .] Dichter hat die beneidenswerte Gabe, mit den schlichtesten und wahrsten und dabei ungemein poetisch wirkenden Worten den erhabenen Frieden des Waldes, wie die mild abgeklärte Ruhe und Ergebenheit zweier alter Leutchen, zu schildern und uns vollständig in den Bann seiner Geschichten zu ziehen: Wald und See und Menschen und der Himmel über ihnen: alles eine einzige wundersame Stimmung" (vol. 6, p. 153),[65] but R. A. Kerr, writing in the *South Atlantic Review*, claimed—inexplicably, by contrast—"[Sharpe's] poems reflect a bleak existential view of life and the nature of human existence [. . .] Such a pessimistic perspective imparts an air of anguish and sadness that penetrates [the] poetry [. . .] These despairing notions are reiterated by persistent allusions to death, disease, thoughts of suicide, and by a morbid vocabulary that makes frequent reference to skulls, corpses, and skeletons. [Sharpe] abandons this lugubrious poetic world only briefly [. . .] in order to make passing observations on the fleeting nature of fame, the shallowness of some political commitments, or the tediousness of life in the business world" (vol. 51, no. 1, p. 157).[66] Paul R. Petrie, writing in *American Literary Realism*, asserted, "The poems range from intensely introspective and/or cryptically metaphysical short lyrics, to pictorial social protest pieces, to longer, philosophical dramatic dialogues";[67] Ellen Davis, in *Agni*, called them "carefully crafted free verse" (no. 44, p. 225);[68] and John Stanley, in *All Ireland Review*, found them to be "sonnets" (vol. 1, no. 24, p. 2).[69] Waclaw Lednicki, in the *American Slavic and East European Review*, wrote, "[Sharpe's] style is marked by an enormous preponderance of nouns with a very frugal use of adjectives," (vol. 4, nos. 3/4, p. 214),[70] while "R. N.," in *Transition*, said that Sharpe "is obviously fascinated by lizards" (no. 1, p. 42).[71] And so on.

The appearance of Sharpe's third collection, *Dazzle Ships*, abruptly inaugurated the third phase of the poet's fame—namely, that of deafening disregard. Not a single review of the new book was published; none, it seems, were submitted for publication; quite probably, none were written.[72] Suddenly and completely,

Sharpe was, like Luise Mühlbach's young Schiller, "shipwrecked on the rock of public indifference."[73]

The fourth and latest vagary of critical opinion was triggered by the arrival of Sharpe's fourth book, *Everything You Hold Dear*. Again, as with the debut collection, the reviewers tumbled over one another to trumpet their valuations publicly; again, the assessments were superabundant and, again, unanimous; this time, however, the tone was one of universal disappointment— if not indeed of hissing, spitting derogation. "As poetry it is not distinguished," said George L. Kline flatly in the *Russian Review* (vol. 22, no. 1, p. 97).[74] "Of high poetical quality," said G. C. Moore Smith in the *Review of English Studies*, "[...] there is little or nothing" (vol. 5, no. 18, p. 219).[75] Said Camillo von Klenze in the *School Review*, "[Here] sometimes sentiment goes over into sentimentality, and in spite of [Sharpe's] health and vigor [Sharpe] becomes tiresome" (vol. 4, no. 8, p. 628).[76] Mary Kinzie in the *American Poetry Review* deplored Sharpe's "tendency [...] to load the poetic work with learning, both historical and metrical, making it almost involuntarily didactic. [...The poems] are generally overburdened by their own accuracy" (vol. 10, no. 6, p. 35).[77] B. C. Thema in *American Anthropologist* complained, "[I]t often taxes the imagination of the reader to follow the meaning of the poems and to read them with understanding and appreciation" (vol. 70, no. 2, p. 410).[78] The "two dozen or so brief poems" in *Everything You Hold Dear* seemed to Terrence N. Hill, writing in the *American Bar Association Journal*, "light stuff. Not unpleasing, but I doubt there is anything here that will send James Dickey into training to defend his title" (vol. 61, no. 2, p. 168).[79] George Monteiro, writing in *American Literature* (and apparently arriving at a different tally), said, "The surprisingly large number of poems gathered up in this [book] will help dispel lack of quantity as a basis for dismissing [Sharpe's] accomplishments"—tartly implying that there were other, sounder bases for dismissal (vol. 66, no. 1, pp. 165–6).[80] Mary

Karr in *Erato* said, "The admiration that one initially feels for [Sharpe's] writing quickly gives way to disrespect for [Sharpe's] sloppy work. [...] The mere fact of selecting poems implies that the cream has been skimmed from a body of work, but in this collection a lot of slop spilled into the pail" (nos. 7/8, p. 13).[81] Dagmar Cäcilia Stern in *German Studies Review*, deprecating the onetime lionization of Sharpe, wrote, "All too often, [...] prizes and public appearances are awarded to writers [...] because they employ conservative, unoriginal, and even banal themes as well as worn-out lyrical structures, while avoiding controversial ideas and deep emotions. Surely such traits in [Sharpe's] poems [...] have contributed to the writer's success. [... Sharpe] is a poet of limited talent with little to offer an American reader—or any reader—in the [first] quarter of the [current] century" (vol. 5, no. 1, p. 139).[82] Horace P. Beck in *Western Folklore,* characterizing the collection, said "[*Everything You Hold Dear*] consists of about seventy pages of Whitmanesque verse that is poetry as we know it only because it is in irregular lines without rhyme or rhythm and is because of these facts extremely hard to follow" (vol. 24, no. 1, p. 54).[83] W. N. Guthrie in the *Sewanee Review*, as if reading a different book, asked rhetorically, "Does not fairness require the statement that a number of short pieces, unfortunately included in the volume, are mere poetic experiments of doubtful value even as such, the feminine rhymes occasionally leading what thought or feeling there is into predicaments which bring it to the brink of nonsense or dissipate it into ghosthood [...?]" (vol. 7, no. 4, p. 500).[84] "Too often," said Jim Ewing in *South Central Review*, with relative leniency, "[Sharpe's] recent work is very uneven" (vol. 4, no. 4, p. 122).[85] Yvor Winters in the *Kenyon Review* was more categorical: "There is much in this book for which I care little, but every poet, I suppose, has a right to his own kinds of failure; at least most poets find them" (vol. 3, no. 4, p. 514).[86] William Archer in his *Poets of the Younger Generation* called the book "insistently monotonous" (p. 412),[87] while the

Encylopaedia Britannica called Sharpe, damningly, "prolific," and lamented that the poems "are vitiated by [their] prevailing Gongorism" (R. S. Peale reprint, vol. IX, p. 33).[88] Eiléan Ní Chuilleanáin in the *Poetry Ireland Review* objected, singularly, that the collection "includes too many finely-observed, even tragically felt, poems about sheep" (no. 46, p. 69).[89] Fellow poets S. Johnson and E. S. V. Millay, respectively, declared the poems "ridiculous beyond the power of satire to exaggerate,"[90] and cruelly observed, "Not only under ground are the brains of men / Eaten by maggots."[91] Perhaps the kindest assessments appeared in a festschrift edition of the *Journal of Canadian Poetry* (vol. 28) dedicated to Sharpe's oeuvre: "[S]imultaneously compelling and mystifying," said Poonam Bajwa (p. 101);[92] "despite moments of inspired observation, much of the second half of [*Everything You Hold Dear*] has the tendency to slip into navel gazing," said Zachary Abram (p. 111);[93] "What I liked about these poems was their remarkable compression," said Paul Harland, before continuing: "[. . .] What I disliked about them was the same thing" (p. 113);[94] Iain Higgins called the latest poems Sharpe's "weakest, with their banal, bourgeois details that cloy rather than concentrate lyrical expression" (p. 124);[95] said Gregory Betts with generous equivocation, "The signature signals the absence of the singer, the word the absence of the world (and author), and the shattered trace is all that remains of the past. Everything becomes fragmented, contingent, situated, infinite, and deeply imponderable—yet the same systems subject to deconstruction carry on their mendacious business apace" (p. 90);[96] "[A]lthough there are some satisfying individual poems [. . .] here," wrote Janice Fiamengo, "the work as a whole has too much the sense of a private conversation" (p. 38);[97] while Neil Besner set the tone early (on page 1) with the judgment, "The prolix [Sharpe] is publishing too much and it is beginning to show."[98] But to go on would be to risk compounding superfluity with incivility. In fine, the critics were unkind.[99]

However, it is to be hoped, and, given the many and violent reversals of opinion over the poet's bright and checkered career, scarcely to be doubted, that—with the publication of *Get Well Soon*, this, Jamie Sharpe's fifth collection of poetry, wherein we find, among others, the startlingly luminous "II," the magnificently bizarre "III," the touchingly apt "IV," the whimsically troubling "VII," the deftly opaque "VIII," the ponderously witty "XI," the stirringly intricate "Doing My Pärt," the amicably taut "The Ship of Theseus," the feverishly articulate "The Crusaders," the soothingly vapid "Half-Life," the tragically wrenching "Short Talks on Anne Carson," and the dramatically puzzling, elegantly plain, archly needling, harrowingly deadpan, mischievously fulsome, lavishly mundane, trickily winsome, devastatingly aloof, spryly poignant, and supernally unsettling "Poetry and the Common Life"— Sharpe's position in the pantheon of letters will undergo yet another whiplash vicissitude.[100]

Notes

1. C. P. Boyko, *En Pointe: The Dance of Life and Literature of Jamie Sharpe* (forthcoming), p. 238.
2. But see Boyko, ibid., pp. 240, 241, 244, 245, 250.
3. See Boyko, ibid., p. 252.
4. For the word "inkle," the authors are indebted to Boyko (ibid., p. 253).
5. Quoted in Boyko, ibid., p. 254.
6. Quoted in Boyko, ibid., p. 255.
7. Quoted in Boyko, ibid., p. 256.
8. Quoted in Boyko, ibid.
9. Quoted in Boyko, ibid., pp. 256–7.
10. Quoted in Boyko, ibid., p. 257.
11. Quoted in Boyko, ibid., p. 258.

12. Quoted in Boyko, ibid.

13. Quoted in Boyko, ibid.

14. Quoted in Boyko, ibid., pp. 259–60, where the following English translation (presumably Boyko's own) also appears: "[Sharpe] is utter master of his language. Whether [Sharpe's] poems are the result of long lucubration or the inspiration of the moment, they bear no mark of effort, and it is not without admiration, nor even without astonishment, that one is carried along—by the noble, unswerving amble of those gorgeous stanzas, proud white hackneys harnessed in gold—into the glory of the evenings. Rich and subtle, [Jamie Sharpe]'s poetry is never merely lyrical; it always encloses an idea within the garland of its metaphors, and however vague or general that idea may be, it serves to strengthen the necklace; the pearls are secured by a thread that, though sometimes invisible, is ever sure."

15. Quoted in Boyko, ibid., p. 260.

16. Quoted in Boyko, ibid., p. 262.

17. Quoted in Boyko, ibid.

18. Quoted in Boyko, ibid.

19. Quoted in Boyko, ibid., p. 263.

20. Quoted in Boyko, ibid.

21. Quoted in Boyko, ibid.

22. Quoted in Boyko, ibid.

23. Quoted in Boyko, ibid., pp. 263–4.

24. Quoted in Boyko, ibid., p. 264.

25. Quoted in Boyko, ibid., p. 265.

26. Quoted in Boyko, ibid., p. 267.

27. For much of the substance, and some of the form, of these two sentences, the authors are indebted to Boyko (ibid., p. 490).

28. Quoted in Boyko, ibid., p. 492.

29. Quoted in Boyko, ibid., p. 493.

30. Quoted in Boyko, ibid.

31. Quoted in Boyko, ibid., p. 495.
32. Quoted in Boyko, ibid.
33. Quoted in Boyko, ibid., p. 496.
34. Quoted in Boyko, ibid., p. 497.
35. Quoted in Boyko, ibid., p. 498.
36. Quoted in Boyko, ibid.
37. Quoted in Boyko, ibid.
38. Quoted in Boyko, ibid.
39. Quoted in Boyko, ibid., p. 501.
40. Quoted in Boyko, ibid.
41. Quoted in Boyko, ibid., p. 502.
42. Quoted in Boyko, ibid., p. 503.
43. Quoted in Boyko, ibid., p. 504.
44. Quoted in Boyko, ibid.
45. Quoted in Boyko, ibid.
46. Quoted in Boyko, ibid., pp. 504–5.
47. Quoted in Boyko, ibid., p. 506.
48. Quoted in Boyko, ibid.
49. Quoted in Boyko, ibid., p. 508.
50. Quoted in Boyko, ibid.
51. Quoted in Boyko, ibid., p. 509.
52. Quoted in Boyko, ibid.
53. Quoted in Boyko, ibid.
54. Quoted in Boyko, ibid., p. 510.
55. Boyko, ibid., p. 512.
56. Quoted in Boyko, ibid., p. 513.
57. Quoted in Boyko, ibid., p. 514.
58. Quoted in Boyko, ibid.
59. Quoted in Boyko, ibid., p. 515.
60. Quoted in Boyko, ibid.
61. Quoted in Boyko, ibid.
62. Quoted in Boyko, ibid., p. 516.
63. Quoted in Boyko, ibid., p. 517.
64. Quoted in Boyko, ibid.

65. Quoted in Boyko, ibid., p. 518, where there also appears this translation (Boyko's?): "This poet has the enviable gift of depicting, in the simplest, truest, and yet artfullest words, the sublime peace of the forest (which is like the mild and mellow calm of a devoted little old couple); we are thereby brought completely under the spell of these stories of woods and ocean and people and the sky above, and drawn entirely in to partake of their paradisiacal mood" (p. 518–9).

66. Quoted in Boyko, ibid., p. 519–20.

67. Quoted in Boyko, ibid., p. 522.

68. Quoted in Boyko, ibid.

69. Quoted in Boyko, ibid.

70. Quoted in Boyko, ibid.

71. Quoted in Boyko, ibid.

72. See Boyko, ibid., pp. 731–49.

73. Translated by Chapman Coleman. Quoted in Boyko, ibid., p. 750.

74. Quoted in Boyko, ibid., p. 981.

75. Quoted in Boyko, ibid.

76. Quoted in Boyko, ibid.

77. Quoted in Boyko, ibid., p. 983.

78. Quoted in Boyko, ibid.

79. Quoted in Boyko, ibid., p. 984.

80. Quoted in Boyko, ibid. The interpretation is Boyko's.

81. Quoted in Boyko, ibid., p. 985.

82. Quoted in Boyko, ibid., p. 986.

83. Quoted in Boyko, ibid.

84. Quoted in Boyko, ibid., p. 988.

85. Quoted in Boyko, ibid.

86. Quoted in Boyko, ibid., p. 989.

87. Quoted in Boyko, ibid.

88. Quoted in Boyko, ibid., p. 990.

89. Quoted in Boyko, ibid., p. 991.

90. Quoted in Boyko, ibid., p. 992.

91. Quoted in Boyko, ibid., p. 993.
92. Quoted in Boyko, ibid.
93. Quoted in Boyko, ibid.
94. Quoted in Boyko, ibid., p. 994.
95. Quoted in Boyko, ibid., p. 995.
96. Quoted in Boyko, ibid.
97. Quoted in Boyko, ibid.
98. Quoted in Boyko, ibid., p. 996.
99. These two sentences are Boyko's (ibid., p. 998).
100. The authors would like to extend their warm gratitude to C. P. Boyko.

Forthcoming from ECW Press:

En Pointe: The Dance of Life

& Literature of Jamie Sharpe

C. P. Boyko

This book is also available as a Global Certified Accessible™ (GCA) ebook. ECW Press's ebooks are screen reader friendly and are built to meet the needs of those who are unable to read standard print due to blindness, low vision, dyslexia, or a physical disability.

At ECW Press, we want you to enjoy our books in whatever format you like. If you've bought a print copy or an audiobook not purchased with a subscription credit, just send an email to ebook@ecwpress.com and include:

- the book title
- the name of the store where you purchased it
- a screenshot or picture of your order/receipt number and your name

A real person will respond to your email with your ePub attached. If you prefer to receive the ebook in PDF format, please let us know in your email.

Some restrictions apply. This offer is only valid for books already available in the ePub format. Some ECW Press books do not have an ePub for us to send you. In those cases, we will let you know if a PDF format is available as an alternative. This offer is only valid for books purchased for personal use. At this time, this program is not offered on school or library copies.

Thank you for supporting an independently owned Canadian publisher with your purchase!